What Babies Think

What **Babies** Think

Penny Gentieu and Tom Friemoth

Andrews McMeel
Publishing

Kansas City

Foreword

Babies are such a mystery. If only we could understand what they are trying to tell us. Does the baby's quizzical, contorted facial expression mean that she is hungry, tired, frustrated . . . or just ready for a nap?

If only we had a clue to what they are really trying to say—if only they could talk! To express themselves so that we could understand what it is they are trying to tell us. Is that giggle because of something cute we did or is it something funny they are thinking about? Is that frown caused by teething pain, a dirty diaper, or just his inability to put thoughts into words?

Although what babies are really thinking will always be a secret, we made some creative guesses for the adorable photos in this book. Of course, there are many possible thoughts, and only the baby knows for sure. We can only sit back and enjoy their charming expressions and gestures.

Penny Gentieu

Tom Friemoth

No photos without my diaper on!

Where's the powder room?

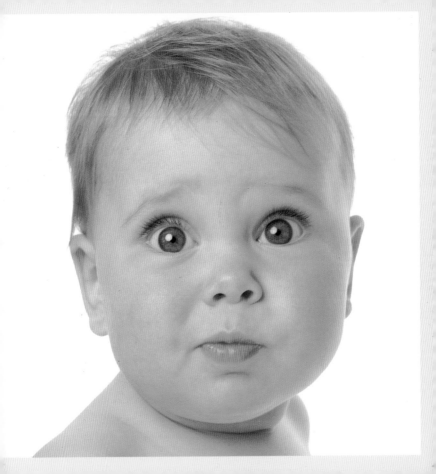

Sure! I'll go to Paris!

Ooooh! So this is the belly button!

You an innie or an outie?

That's nothing!
One night I went through
three cans of formula!

I want to
be a doctor
and that's final.

I wish I could do that!

Flash cards
already?

Okay . . .
next!

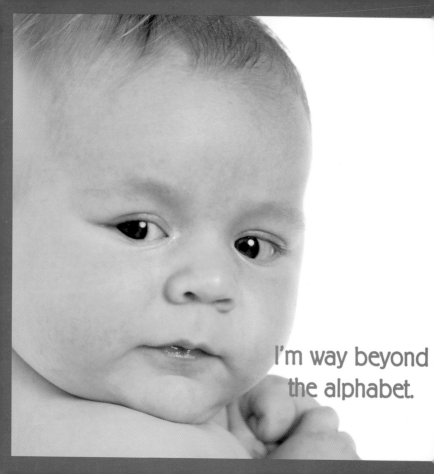

I'm way beyond
the alphabet.

Let me see, that's 1, 2, 3, 4, 5

Keep rubbing my toes!

You're a good mom.

I can't think of
one thing I have
to do today!

Hello, Baby!

Are you
married?

A playdate with Suzie?
YES!

Dad, can you teach ME how to wiggle my ears?

This must be love!

If I hear goo-goo one more time I'll . . .

Not blue
eyeliner!

Look at the size of
that mouse!

It wasn't me!

She was looking at me
with those big baby blue eyes and . . .

Your old baby stories
are so (yawn)
exciting.

I don't want to know what you heard at the hairdresser's.

Tell me more!

She did
what?

I'm speechless.

Okay, I'm up, now what?

I'm not.

I'm not saying another word!

If you could read my mind . . .

Give me a minute.
I'll figure it out.

Boy, what I wouldn't give!

I can't remember what I had for breakfast.

I see a mountain of ice cream
with chocolate sprinkles, M&M's . . .

Mom, do you remember your good vase?

Board books are for babies.

What's that you're wearing on your head?

That's

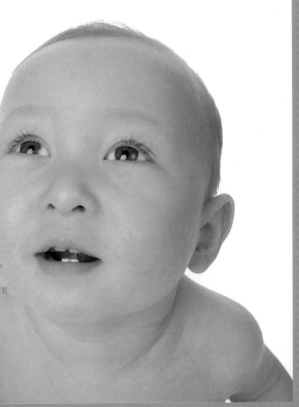

E

F P

T O Z

L P E D

P E C F D

E D F C Z P

E L G P E D O L

D O C E P L D E

Ooo eee baby!

I'm pretending I'm a cat!

I'm serious about wanting my bottle

Now I KNOW
I don't like broccoli.

Bring on the Cheerios!

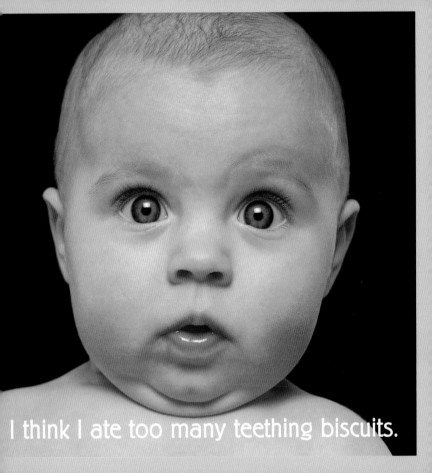

I think I ate too many teething biscuits.

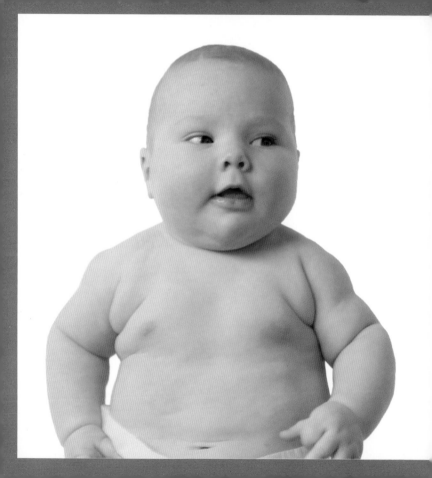

You name it, I'll eat it.

Ahh . . . there's nothing like a good burp!

Pass me
that football!

Go ahead,
I can catch it!

Wherever did you find this thing?

All that for me?

Okay, I'm ready! FEED ME!

A somewhat
smoky taste
with a hint of
currants . . .

Too much pepper.

Thumbs taste good!

I prefer fingers.

It's really good! Here—try one!

Mom, I got that fly.

Turn right, go down two blocks, and it's the one with the toys in the window.